TONGUES
Interpretation
&
PROPHECY

TONGUES
Interpretation
&
PROPHECY

Don
BASHAM

WHITAKER
HOUSE

Tongues, Interpretation & Prophecy

ISBN: 978-1-60374-767-7
eBook ISBN: 978-1-60374-768-4
Printed in the United States of America
© 1971, 2012 by Whitaker House

Whitaker House
1030 Hunt Valley Circle
New Kensington, PA 15068
www.whitakerhouse.com

Library of Congress Cataloging-in-Publication Data (pending)

This book has been printed digitally and produced in a standard specification in order to ensure its continuing availability.

TABLE OF CONTENTS

INTRODUCTION

Two years ago, *A Handbook on Holy Spirit Baptism* was published, intended primarily as a help to those attending seminars where the baptism and gifts of the Holy Spirit were being taught. To our delight, it seemed to find a particular niche in the literary market, and its reception has far exceeded our expectations.

But *A Handbook on Holy Spirit Baptism* dealt almost entirely with the initial experience of the baptism in the Holy Spirit, and the people helped by it began to ask why a similar handbook on questions and answers on the other gifts of the Holy Spirit could not be provided. Since the first handbook seemed a convenient size, it was decided that a second handbook would be produced, rather than enlarging and revising the first.

Tongues, Interpretation & Prophecy is the result. Like the first in the series, it follows a simple question and answer format and does not require reading from beginning to end to be of value. Once more we have allowed the question itself to serve as the chapter heading. Thus, by referring to the table of contents, you can quickly find those questions of greatest interest to you.

If the Holy Spirit chooses to bless and prosper this second handbook as He did the first, I shall be more than grateful and more than satisfied.

—Don W. Basham

SECTION I

CONCERNING SPIRITUAL GIFTS

"Now concerning spiritual gifts, brethren, I would not have you ignorant."
—1 Corinthians. 12:1

CHAPTER 1

Why do you divide the nine gifts of the Holy Spirit into three
categories of three gifts each?

In 1 Corinthians chapter twelve, Paul listed the nine spiritual manifestations we have come to call the nine gifts of the Holy Spirit.

> *For to one is given by the Spirit the word of wisdom; to another*
> *the word of knowledge by the same Spirit; to another faith by*
> *the same Spirit; to another the gifts of healing by the same*
> *Spirit; to another the working of miracles; to another proph-*
> *ecy; to another discerning of spirits; to another divers kinds of*
> *tongues; to another the interpretation of tongues: but all these*
> *worketh that one and the selfsame Spirit, dividing to every*
> *man severally as he will.*   (1 Corinthians 12:8–11)

For many years, biblical scholars have recognized that by their definition as well as their function, these manifestations or "gifts" clearly fall into three categories of three gifts each. There are three gifts of inspiration, three gifts of revelation, and three gifts of power.

Gifts of Inspiration:
   Tongues

Interpretation of Tongues
Prophecy

Gifts of Revelation:
Word of Knowledge
Word of Wisdom
Discerning of Spirits

Gifts of Power:
Faith
Healings
Miracles

As indicated by its title, this book addresses itself primarily to questions dealing with the inspirational gifts; tongues, interpretation of tongues, and prophecy. Subsequent handbooks will deal with the gifts of revelation and the gifts of power.

The gifts of inspiration have also been referred to as the *vocal* gifts, since in order for their manifestation, there must be utilization of the vocal or speech apparatus of the person through whom they are being manifested. This is not necessarily the case with the gifts of revelation or the gifts of power.

CHAPTER 2

*What is the difference between the gifts of the Holy Spirit
that Paul listed in 1 Corinthians 12:8–10 and the ministries
he listed in 1 Corinthians 12:28–30?*

The confusion between the gifts of the Holy Spirit and the ministries of the Holy Spirit has caused no little problem among Christians. Essentially, the gifts or manifestations of the Holy Spirit in 1 Corinthians 12:8–10 are supernatural gifts resident in the Holy Spirit that may be distributed to various persons. They can be characterized as momentary rather than continuing. Theoretically, any person baptized in the Holy Spirit can manifest any or all of these gifts.

Since they are momentary, they do not become the "possession" of any person. It is inaccurate for someone to say, "I have three gifts of the Holy Spirit" simply because he may have manifested at one time or another three gifts of the Holy Spirit.

To use a personal illustration, a number of the nine gifts have appeared in my own ministry. On occasion, I have had the gift of tongues that someone else interpreted. Later, I prophesied. Another time, I gave an interpretation of tongues. In each case, it was a gift of the Holy Spirit, not *my* gift.

But these *gifts* are not the same as the five *ministries* listed at the end of 1 Corinthians 12. The fact that I manifested the gift of tongues in a meeting does not mean that I have a *ministry* of speaking in tongues. Nor does the fact that I pray for someone's healing mean that I have a *ministry* of healing. In 1 Corinthians 12:28–30 Paul was saying that God has set certain ministries in the church. But he made it plain that not everyone will have the same ministry.

"*Are all apostles? Are all prophets?*" he asked. Meaning of course, no. So then, the fact that a man may prophesy does not mean his *ministry* will be that of a prophet, or because he interprets a tongue that he will have a *ministry* of interpretation.

For example, Oral Roberts has been set into the church with a *ministry* of healing, but this does not prevent him from prophesying. Nor does the fact that I do not have a *ministry* of healing prevent me from praying successfully, on occasion, for the sick. In fact, one of the nine gifts of the Spirit may operate through me a number of times without my being given a ministry by that name. (However, repeated manifestations of a specific gift *may* indicate God's intention for that person to fulfill that ministry.)

The nine gifts are distributed by the Holy Spirit as need demands. The ministries are offices God has set in the church to be filled by various persons. Two Scriptures about prophecy, linked together, show the distinction. In 1 Corinthians 12:30, Paul said, "*Are all prophets?*" meaning, no, all are not prophets. Yet in 1 Corinthians 14:31, he said, "*For **you may all prophesy** one by one, that all may learn, and all may be encouraged.*" So the gift of prophecy operating through a man does not necessarily make him a prophet.

CHAPTER 3

What is the difference between spiritual gifts and man's talents?

A clear distinction needs to be made between *talents*, which are the natural abilities a man is born with, and *spiritual gifts*, which are *supernatural* manifestations of God's power provided by the Holy Spirit. Unfortunately, some of the modern translations of the Scriptures—edited by scholars who have no experience with the charismatic gifts—tend to suffer from that lack of experience. It is not difficult for a man who doubts the validity of biblical miracles to call prophecy "inspired preaching," or speaking in tongues "ecstatic utterance." There has been a longstanding tendency among such scholars to "demythologize" the Scriptures, to substitute natural explanations for supernatural events, and natural abilities for supernatural gifts.

When a man with certain natural talents becomes a Christian, he will probably attempt to redirect those talents into Christian channels. For example, a nightclub singer who has been converted may become a Christian vocalist for some evangelist. Or a converted lawyer may become a brilliant preacher. But neither the singing ability of the vocalist, nor the eloquence of the lawyer can be considered "spiritual gifts." They are merely redirected human talents.

Spiritual gifts, on the other hand, are the direct result of the Holy Spirit's *supernatural* activity in a person, providing him with gifts or abilities completely separate from any natural proclivity.

I know a woman in Pennsylvania who had no natural musical ability at all. But after she was baptized in the Holy Spirit, she began to receive songs in the Spirit, both words and music. Some have been published and have been a great blessing to many people. By her own admission, the songs came directly out of her communion and worship.

Anyone, Christian or non-Christian, may have talent. But the true gifts of the Holy Spirit are made available only to those "twice-born" men and women who are consciously participating in the supernatural life of Jesus Christ.

Paul contrasted the difference between the natural (although talented) man and the Christian in these two passages.

And my speech and my preaching was not with enticing words of man's wisdom, but in the demonstration of the Spirit and of power: that your faith should not stand in the wisdom of men, but in the power of God. (1 Corinthians 2:4–5)

But the natural man receiveth not the things of the Spirit of God: for they are foolishness unto him: neither can he know them, for they are spiritually discerned. (1 Corinthians 2:14)

CHAPTER 4

Can a person have spiritual gifts without being baptized in the Holy Spirit?

Since the Scripture says, *"With God all things are possible"* (Matthew 19:26), we must admit that any Christian could—if God so willed—manifest a spiritual gift. After all, God made even Balaam's donkey speak. And I have known of exceptional and rare instances where Christians unfamiliar with the baptism in the Holy Spirit have manifested gifts normally associated only with those who have been baptized in the Holy Spirit.

But generally speaking, the nine gifts of the Holy Spirit Paul listed in 1 Corinthians 12 seem to be reserved for those Christians who have received the baptism in the Holy Spirit.

Both conversion and baptism in the Holy Spirit can be called doorway experiences. The non-Christian meets the Lord Jesus Christ in a conversion experience, is born again, and begins to enjoy the privileges of one born into the kingdom of God. He has moved from one realm to another. Then, the same Christian receives the baptism in the Holy Spirit, moving into still a deeper realm of supernatural experience.

The spiritual principle is this: we receive only out of the realm we are in. If non-Christian, we receive only from that realm. If a

born-again believer in Jesus Christ, we receive the provision that realm offers. Once baptized in the Holy Spirit, we can receive supernatural gifts of the Spirit unavailable to the Christian not baptized in the Holy Spirit.

As a result of the teaching ministry I've been in for the past several years, I have traveled extensively in the United States and in a number of foreign countries as well. And I would have to say that out of the thousands of people with whom I have had fellowship, I have found no church, no fellowship group, no house prayer meeting, and no individual Christian manifesting the nine gifts of the Holy Spirit except those who were baptized in the Holy Spirit.

I'm not saying there aren't any such groups or individuals; only that I have not met them. And I believe any such group or individual would be an exception to the established biblical principle that it is not conversion, but the baptism in the Holy Spirit, that introduces people to the realm where supernatural gifts and ministries abound.

CHAPTER 5

Why do so many Spirit-baptized Christians experience only the gift of speaking in tongues? Why don't they move on into other gifts?

This is an important question and one that I trust this book will help provide the answer to. Dozens of times in charismatic seminars across the country, I have taken a simple poll. In a congregation of, say, two hundred fifty, I will ask for a show of hands of all those who are baptized in the Holy Spirit with the evidence of speaking in tongues. Perhaps two hundred people will raise their hands.

Then I will ask, "How many of you Spirit-baptized Christians who just raised your hands have ever brought a message in tongues to be interpreted, have ever given an interpretation, or have ever prophesied?" Out of two hundred fifty, perhaps thirty people will raise their hands.

In other words, six out of seven Spirit-baptized Christians have never manifested any gift of the Holy Spirit beside their devotional tongue. Why?

I believe there are two main reasons. One is ignorance—ignorance about the other gifts of the Holy Spirit and how they operate in the believer's life. The other reason is fear. Spirit-baptized

Christians have been much too timid in moving on into the other spiritual gifts. This book's purpose is to help remedy both these difficulties.

CHAPTER 6

A minister who is being genuinely used to minister spiritual gifts is known by some of us to be living in immorality. Why does God continue to honor his ministry with miracles?

Disturbing as it is, such a thing can and does happen. And while to give a detailed answer to this tragic problem is outside the scope of this book, the pressing reality of such situations among us— and the problem is becoming increasingly prevalent—demands we acknowledge and answer it, even if only briefly.

The charismatic community in the body of Christ today needs to be made aware of a little-recognized spiritual truth. Namely, that *the presence of supernatural gifts in a man's ministry must not be taken as evidence of divine approval of his ethics or morals.* It's a matter of understanding what the Scriptures teach about both the *gifts* and the *fruit* of the Holy Spirit.

The gifts of the Holy Spirit reflect nothing about the character of a man, other than the fact that he has faith in the power of God. Spiritual gifts represent the supernatural ability of God flowing through a human channel. That's why we call them *gifts.* A gift, by its very definition, says much about the giver, but nothing about the worth or character of the one receiving the gift. Supernatural gifts of the Holy Spirit reflect the love and benevolence of a God who desires to minister supernaturally to the needs of His children. But the human channel through whom those gifts flow may not only be imperfect, he may even be immoral.

We have made the mistake of assuming that if a man can prophesy or cast out demons in the name of Jesus, then he must be of sterling moral worth. But that is man's *assumption*, a false assumption that is not borne out in Scripture.

The scriptural measure of whether a man is a true or false prophet is not the content of his message or ministry, but the presence of the *fruit* of the Spirit in his life.

Jesus said, *"Beware of false prophets, which come to you in sheep's clothing, but inwardly they are ravening wolves. **Ye shall know them by their fruits**"* (Matthew 7:15–16). (Not by their gifts!) Unfortunately, the number of false prophets preying on the people of God today is on the increase.

As Rev. Derek Prince has frequently said, "If you want to know whether a man is a true or false prophet, don't judge by the miracles in his ministry. See rather if he pays his bills and whose wife he's traveling with."

Pastor H. M. Maxwell-Whyte, a man gifted in the ministry of casting out demons, has commented on this same truth. "I have often told my people to keep their eyes off the human channel and on Jesus Christ," he says, "for the authority and power are in Jesus Christ and not in me. I could commit some gross act of immorality in the afternoon and then come into the church sanctuary that evening and cast out demons in the name of Jesus Christ."

But unfortunately many Christians have been so blinded by the powerful *gifts* of the Holy Spirit that may operate in a man's life that they fail to see, or they ignore, the fruit or immorality and dishonesty that identify the man as a false prophet.

I think we can assume that practically every man begins his ministry in Christ honestly and faithfully. Then he becomes "gifted" by faith in the supernatural power of God and people begin to be blessed by his ministry. His success puts him in the way of many more temptations than he knew before. He succumbs to temptation, and immorality and dishonesty begin to creep into his life. To his surprise, the miracles still flow through his ministry. He becomes deceived, and the people to whom he ministers are deceived, assuming that the miracles are proof of his personal holiness.

But they are not. They are simply the evidence that God is continuing to honor *His* word, to manifest *His* love in a supernatural way to meet the needs of *His* people. Paul reminded us, "*The gifts and the call of God are irrevocable*" (Romans 11:29 rsv). And God has bound Himself to His Word, to fulfill it.

I may wonder why God does it the way He does. If I were God, I might have chosen to do it another way. I might have snatched the gifts away from a man the very moment he stepped out of line. But then, my way is not God's way. The Scripture shows us God's way, and God's way is that He will honor *His* word and perform *His* work.

Paul said, "*Be not deceived, God is not mocked: for whatsoever a man soweth, that shall he also reap*" (Galatians 6:7). If a man whose ministry is being blessed by the supernatural gifts of God decides, in the midst of his ministry, to "sow to his own flesh," he will from the flesh eventually "*reap corruption,*" and destroy himself. (See verse 8).

But in the meantime God will protect the integrity of the gifts for the gifts belong to Him and not to the one ministering them.

SECTION II

SPEAKING IN TONGUES

"Now I want you all to speak in tongues…"
—1 Corinthians 14:5 RSV

CHAPTER 7

Is everyone supposed to speak in tongues?

If it is the will of God for every Christian to receive the baptism in the Holy Spirit (and I believe it is), and if we are correct in believing that every Spirit-baptized Christian should have the biblical evidence of speaking in tongues, then of course, the answer to the question is yes.

I believe the Scriptures confirm this. Paul said, *"Now I want you **all** to speak in tongues"* (1 Corinthians 14:5 RSV, emphasis added). Here Paul was referring to the ability to speak in tongues that comes when one received the baptism in the Holy Spirit. He was referring to the same ability when he said, *"I thank God that I speak in tongues more than you all"* (1 Corinthians 14:18 RSV).

There is overwhelming evidence in the book of Acts confirming the fact that speaking in tongues is the normal, expected sign or proof that one has received the baptism in the Holy Spirit. In the five accounts in the book of Acts where the Holy Spirit is received, four of the five indicated that the people receiving the Holy Spirit ended up speaking in tongues. If you want a more detailed discussion of speaking in tongues as the evidence of the baptism, you can read the chapter entitled, "Tongues: The Primary Evidence" in *Ministering the Baptism in the Holy Spirit.*[1]

---

1. Don W. Basham, *Ministering the Baptism in the Holy Spirit,* Whitaker House, New Kensington, PA, 1971, pp. 28–42.

Occasionally, Christians who believe they have received the baptism in the Holy Spirit complain to me that they have not received tongues and see no need to. We cannot dogmatically say that everyone must speak in tongues in order to have the baptism, but we merely point out that it is the *normal* experience.

It is said that the baptism in the Holy Spirit is the doorway into the supernatural realm of the Christian life. And since speaking in tongues is a supernatural way of praying, it is often considered the doorway to the other supernatural gifts, such as interpretation and prophecy.

I believe this is the reason Paul said, *"I want you all to speak in tongues, but even more to prophesy"* (1 Corinthians 14:5). He put speaking in tongues—the initial supernatural manifestation—first, then lead into prophecy.

Why should every Christian speak in tongues? I appreciate the answer of Rev. Ernie Gruen, a pastor in Kansas City, Kansas: "Speaking in tongues is the prayer part of the baptism in the Holy Spirit," Ernie says. "To miss speaking in tongues is to miss God's miraculous provision, enabling you to pray with supernatural effectiveness."

And to those who claim that the baptism can be received without tongues, Ernie Gruen gives this delightful testimony.

"Maybe the baptism in the Holy Spirit can be received without tongues, but that's not for me. When I began seeking the baptism, I told the Lord I wanted it just the way the apostles received it—tongues and all. If I hadn't received the evidence of tongues, I wouldn't have been sure I had the baptism. My prayer to God was like this:

Lord, if I don't get what the apostles got
The way they got what they got,
Then I won't know that I got what they got.

But Lord, if I get what they got
The way they got what they got,
Then I'll know I got what they got.

And Ernie Gruen's glad testimony is, "I got what they got!"

CHAPTER 8

Is everyone who prays in tongues
supposed to have the gift of tongues?

A clear distinction must be made between the ability to *pray* in tongues that one receives when he is baptized in the Holy Spirit, and the *gift* of tongues (actually, kinds of tongues) that Paul listed along with the other eight gifts of the Holy Spirit.

We believe that everyone receiving the baptism in the Holy Spirit can and should receive tongues and exercise this supernatural way of praying every day. It is the one supernatural manifestation given primarily for the edification of the individual believer. The other gifts of the Spirit, including tongues, are gifts to the church for building up the church. This is why Paul said, *"He who speaks in a tongue edifies himself, but he who prophesies edifies the church"* (1 Corinthians 14:4 RSV).

Having personally experienced praying in tongues and the strength it provides, Paul could gratefully acknowledge, *"I thank God that I speak in tongues more than you all"* (1 Corinthians 14:18, RSV, and in the Greek, "more than you all put together"). But then acknowledging the importance of prophecy and interpretation *in the church*, in order that the whole congregation might benefit from spiritual manifestations, Paul added, *"Nevertheless, **in church** I* *would rather speak five words with my mind, in order to instruct others, than ten thousand words in a tongue"* (1 Corinthians 14:19 RSV).

Therefore, we see that tongues used in private devotions fall in one category, while tongues (kinds of tongues) manifested in the public worship service and followed by the gift of interpretation, fall in another category.

Should everyone who prays in tongues exercise the gift of tongues?

We pointed out in Chapter 5 how only one out of every six or seven people who are baptized in the Holy Spirit have ever manifested the gift of tongues (kinds of tongues) where interpretation should follow. But while this is how things *are*, we don't believe this is how things *should* be. While everyone who *prays* in tongues doesn't manifest the *gift* of tongues, we believe that anyone desiring the *gift* of tongues can manifest it.

We have already noted that all nine gifts are resident in the Holy Spirit and that any Spirit-baptized believer has the nine gifts available to him, potentially. Therefore, a much higher percentage than one out of six or seven persons should be manifesting the *gift* of tongues. And as we come to understand the ways in which we can press into the spiritual gifts, many more will.

CHAPTER 9

What is the difference between new tongues, other tongues,
tongues, kinds of tongues, and unknown tongues?

Two years ago, I was speaking to a small group of American missionaries in Austria. It was the night before some of us were to make a sojourn into Yugoslavia and Hungary to smuggle in some literature and to have fellowship with the Christians in those beleaguered countries. Of the group I was addressing, some were baptized in the Holy Spirit and some were not. I talked for about an hour, describing the charismatic movement in the United States and sharing from the Word of God about the gifts of the Holy Spirit.

One Baptist missionary took issue with what I said, especially about the manifestation of speaking in tongues. He had a carefully worked out exposition of the Scriptures in defense of his belief that speaking in tongues is not for today.

"I received the baptism in the Holy Spirit when I was converted," he insisted. "And since that time I have been witnessing for Christ with the 'new tongue' Jesus prophesied believers would have. (See Mark 16:17.) When I was converted, the Holy Spirit gave me a new, Christian way of talking to people.

"Speaking in other tongues, as the apostles did on the day of Pentecost, in languages that were understandable to those who listened, was an experience that was never repeated," the missionary argued, "and the unknown tongues Paul talked about in Corinthians are not the same as the phenomenon that occurred at Pentecost. The Corinthian tongues were gibberish that no one understood and that had to be interpreted."

I quote the missionary's remarks since they represent a point of view very widespread among Christians who do not yet understand the revival of the gifts of the Holy Spirit appearing in the church today. But before we answer the missionary's statements, let us quote the passages that mention the various types of tongues.

New Tongues

*These signs shall follow them that believe; in my name shall they cast out devils; they shall speak with **new tongues**.*

(Mark 16:17)

Other Tongues

*And they were all filled with the Holy Ghost and began to speak with **other tongues**, as the Spirit gave them utterance... And they [the multitudes] were all amazed and marvelled, saying to one another, Behold, are not all these which speak Galilaeans? And how hear we every man in our own tongue, wherein we were born?* (Acts 2:4, 7–8)

Tongues

*While Peter yet spake these words, the Holy Ghost fell on all them which heard the word. And they of the circumcision which believed were astonished, as many as came with Peter, because that on the Gentiles also was poured out the gift of the Holy Ghost. For they heard them speak with **tongues**, and magnify God.* (Acts 10:44-46)

Kinds of Tongues

*For to one is given by the Spirit the word of wisdom; to another the word of knowledge by the same Spirit; to another faith by the same Spirit; to another the gifts of healing by the same Spirit; to another the working of miracles; to another prophecy; to another discerning of Spirits, to another divers **kinds of tongues**; to another the interpretation of tongues.*

(1 Corinthians 12:8–10)

Unknown Tongues

*For he that speaketh in an **unknown tongue** speaketh not unto men, but unto God....He that speaketh in an **unknown tongue** edifieth himself.* (1 Corinthians 14:2, 4)

Complicated theories about spiritual gifts by those who have not experienced them are common. The liberal churchman with no personal conversion experience has an altogether different explanation of what it means to be "born again" than the soundly converted believer who *knows* his sins are forgiven and that he's "saved."

By the same token, the evangelical Christian who has not experienced speaking in tongues will offer quite a different explanation of the Scriptures that deal with that phenomenon from the Spirit-baptized Christian.

New Tongues

The missionary's claim that the *"new tongues"* in Mark 16:17 are simply a description of Christian conversation does violence both to the context of the Scripture and the experience of speaking in tongues. Many biblical scholars agree that the *"new tongues"* prophesied by Jesus are identical to the *"other tongues"* that the apostles spoke on the day of Pentecost. Certainly, no Christian baptized in the Holy Spirit and who knows the benefits of praying in tongues would feel any necessity to strain the Scriptures by any such far-fetched interpretation. In addition, the passage not only refers to the miraculous sign of speaking in tongues, but also refers to casting out demons and healing; charismatic ministries that are equally foreign to the average evangelical Christian.

Other Tongues

As to the claim that the *"other tongues"* in Acts 2:4, which were understood by the hearers, were a once-for-all, non-repeatable experience, the facts clearly indicate this is not true. Many times today, the "other tongues" spoken by Spirit-baptized Christians are foreign languages heard and understood by persons present. Chapter 14 of this book describes a series of such events.

Tongues

Since no one recognized the tongues spoken at the house of Cornelius in Acts 10, it is said they are not the same as the *"other tongues"* spoken on the Day of Pentecost. But the fact that the *"tongues"* in Acts 10 are the same as the *"other tongues"* in Acts 2 is made plain by the Scriptures themselves. Both are the tongues that appear as the evidence that the baptism of the Holy Spirit has been received.

First, the Jewish believers who accompanied Peter to Cornelius' home recognized that the Gentiles had received the Holy Spirit specifically *because* they heard them speaking in tongues. (See Acts 10:45–46.) And Peter himself equated the experience of those Gentile Christians receiving the Holy Spirit with his own experience at Pentecost, for when he reports the incident to the Christians back at Jerusalem he admits as much. *"And as I began to speak, **the Holy Ghost fell on them, as on us at the beginning**"* (Acts 11:15).

Therefore we see that *"other tongues"* in Acts 4:2 and *"tongues"* in Acts 11:15 refer to the same kind of experience. The fact that the tongues went unrecognized at the house of Cornelius made no difference to Peter. After all, he himself had not understood the languages he and the 120 spoke on the day of Pentecost. It had been the multitude that gathered who had recognized the languages.

Kinds of Tongues

In his reference to "kinds of tongues" as one of the nine gifts of the Holy Spirit, Paul indicated this manifestation differs from the ones mentioned in Acts, in that it is to be used in the public worship services of the church, to be followed by the companion gift of interpretation.

Unknown Tongues

When the word *"unknown"* appears with the word tongues, as it does in several places in 1 Corinthians 12 and 14 in the King James Version, you will note the word is in italics. This simply indicates that the word does not appear in the Greek manuscripts and was inserted by the translators. From the context we see that Paul, in these passages, was referring both to the gift of "kinds of tongues" and to the devotional tongue with which one can pray and worship God—the tongue that was given as the evidence of the baptism in the Holy Spirit. This is clear in 1 Corinthians 14:27–28.

> *If any man speak in an unknown tongue, let it be by two, or at the most three, and that by course, and let one interpret.*

Here, Paul was speaking of "kinds of tongues," which are to be interpreted.

> *But if there be no interpreter, let him keep silence in the church; and let him speak [in tongues] to himself, and to God.*

Here, Paul was referring to the devotional tongue.

Experience shows that the actual process of speaking in tongues is the same; whether new tongues, other tongues, tongues, kinds of tongues, or unknown tongues. The application determines which category it falls in, and what restrictions, if any, are placed on its use.

CHAPTER 10

Is speaking in tongues always in a known language, even though no one present understands what is being spoken?

The question reflects the doubts of many people newly-baptized in the Holy Spirit. They speak in tongues but are not fully enjoying the blessings of praying "in the Spirit" because of the doubts harassing them; doubts as to whether the tongues they are speaking are "real" tongues; that is, actual languages.

I went through the same period of doubting when I was baptized in the Holy Spirit. Most people do. I was a student in Bible college, and no one warned me that Satan would try to rob me of my experience by making me doubt the reality of tongues.

I was studying New Testament Greek at the time, and would pore over the vocabulary section of my Greek text book, earnestly trying to find some "real" Greek words that sounded like what I was saying in tongues. I felt if I could confirm that I was actually praying in a real language known to someone somewhere, it would give me the assurance I sought that what I was doing was genuine. I know now that 95 percent of the people receiving the baptism in the Holy Spirit have some doubts about their experience of speaking in tongues, at least at first.

Actually, the Scriptures indicate the possibility that speaking in tongues can be either a known language or some form of "angelic speech." Paul said, "*If I speak in the tongues of men **and of angels***" (1 Corinthians 13:1 RSV). And he also said, "*For one who speaks in a tongue speaks not to men but to God; for **no one** understands him, but he utters mysteries in the Spirit*" (1 Corinthians 14:2 RSV).

Certainly then, we must allow the possibility that some tongues may be in a language known no place on this earth. The point to remember is that even if this is true, it in no way denies the validity of speaking in tongues.

Some critics claim that the tongues Paul spoke of in his first Corinthian letter—tongues that need the gift of interpretation to be understood—are altogether different from the foreign languages spoken on the day of Pentecost. They say the Corinthian tongues were not languages at all, but meaningless gibberish. They claim as well that all so-called speaking in tongues by Christians today falls into this category. Most Spirit-baptized Christians have heard this criticism in one form or another and it has contributed to their doubts about their own speaking in tongues. But here is where personal experience gives added understanding to what the Scriptures are saying. The Christian who tries to explain the supernatural experiences described in the New Testament without personal experience of such things will inevitably have a different—and inadequate—understanding of Scriptures that describe such experiences.

A man I know was the speaker at a Christian meeting. At one point he stopped his message and began speaking in tongues. This was immediately followed by an interpretation of the tongue by someone in the audience. Then the man resumed his message. After the service, a Frenchman came up to the speaker and told him that the message in tongues was in the French language and that the interpretation that followed had been a perfect translation in English of what had been spoken in French. But neither the speaker nor the interpreter knew any French.

Such an experience amounts to a combination of what took place on the day of Pentecost, when people heard and understood the languages spoken by the 120, and of what Paul described in 1 Corinthians, where the gift of tongues was to be followed by the gift of interpretation.

So whether the *"unknown"* tongues in which we pray are comprised of earthly languages spoken by men somewhere on earth, or angelic speech that can be translated only in heaven and require the gift of interpretation to be understood anywhere on earth, they remain an authentic and precious gift of God.

CHAPTER 11

How do you answer those people who say speaking in tongues is of the devil?

This question has added pertinence in light of the vast increase in Satanic activity in our culture today. There are two things we want to make crystal clear as we answer this question, however.

1. There is a Satanic counterfeit for every gift of the Holy Spirit, including speaking in tongues.

2. But no Christian need have any fear of receiving the counterfeit from Satan if he is seeking the genuine gifts of the Holy Spirit in a scripturally-approved manner.

Let us look at Satan's counterfeit first. We live in an age when Satan is pouring out a counterfeit Pentecost comprised of all kinds of fascinating supernatural phenomena, such as fortune-telling, witchcraft, astrology, ESP, spiritualism, black magic, drugs, hypnotism, psychic healing, and the like. And many Christians have deliberately gotten involved in these black arts, thus exposing themselves to demonic invasion.

Since demons are living (though invisible) personalities with wills of their own, and can exercise a measure of control even in a Christian's life, under certain circumstances, they can manifest themselves in such a way as to deceive the ignorant into believing their antics are evidences of the Holy Spirit.

In Pennsylvania some time back, I was teaching on the gifts of the Holy Spirit. After the service a nervous, bespectacled young man sought to talk to me.

"I already have the baptism in the Holy Spirit," he said. "But when I speak in tongues, it sounds funny. It doesn't sound like other people's tongues. And I feel real depressed afterward. Can you help me?"

"Maybe you just need to become more fluent in your praying," I replied. "Let's worship God together for a few minutes, praying in the Spirit, so I can listen to you."

He nodded and we began to pray. As I watched, his face took on a strained expression and hoarse, guttural sounds began to issue forth from his mouth. Sensing that what was manifesting itself was not the Holy Spirit, I said, "You strange spirit, I command you in the name of Jesus Christ to loose this man and come out!"

The results were immediate and explosive. The youth fell on the floor and let out a prolonged wail. Then he relaxed. Slowly he got to his feet. "W-What was that?"

"That was a demonic spirit, and we commanded it to leave. How do you feel?"

"Kinda funny," he admitted. "But clean inside. And I don't feel shaky anymore."

"Good. Now let's pray that Jesus will give you the genuine article, the real baptism in the Holy Spirit."

We prayed, and joy spread over his face as he began praising God fluently in a clear heavenly language. Afterward he told me a typical story of involvement in drugs, witchcraft, and Eastern cults.

Then he had found Christ, and after learning of the baptism in the Holy Spirit, had begun seeking it on his own in times of quiet meditation. Because of his demonic bondage, he had been unable to receive. However, a demon had obliged with strange manifestations, which made him think he was speaking in tongues.

But let us make one thing clear. What happened was not a result of his seeking the baptism in the Holy Spirit, but of demonic activity already present in his life. Once delivered from the spirit manifesting the counterfeit, he could receive the real thing.

So we see there is a counterfeit of speaking in tongues just as there is a counterfeit of prophecy and healing and other genuine spiritual gifts. *But no Christian seeking the baptism in the Holy Spirit with speaking in tongues needs to be afraid.* When we ask in the name of Jesus, what we get, we get from God. If in the process of our seeking, the Holy Spirit reveals some demonic influence and we get rid of that, so much the better.

Some people claim speaking in tongues is of the devil because of a "dispensationalist" theology that says the age of miracles is past. Those who embrace this theology have to find some explanation for the miraculous gifts of the Holy Spirit reappearing in the church today. Since their theology doesn't allow God to perform miracles today, the miracles must come from Satan. Unfortunately, those exposed to this false theology become instilled with fear that makes it difficult for them to ever receive the supernatural things of God.

When I was in New Zealand recently, I had the privilege of seeing several hundred people receive the baptism in the Holy Spirit with the evidence of speaking in tongues. Among them were some members of the Church of The Brethren, a small conservative denomination whose doctrine precludes miracles. One of their ministers came to me after he and some of his people had received the baptism. There were tears of joy in his eyes and impulsively he embraced me in a bear hug.

"Brother Basham, I can't tell you how much this means to me," he said. "You see, our church teaches that speaking in tongues is of the devil. I grew up in my denomination and from the time I was a small boy, I had that teaching pounded into my head. As the Holy Spirit began moving powerfully in the churches here in New Zealand, and some of our Christian friends in other denominations began to receive the baptism in the Holy Spirit, we were continually warned to 'Stay away from those Pentecostals. What they are doing is from the devil!'

"And even when my own study of the Scriptures convinced me that our doctrinal position was wrong and I began to seek the baptism, I still had to contend with those terrible fears instilled in me in my childhood."

Perhaps the best Scripture for those who, because of this kind of false teaching, are fearful that tongues may be of the devil, is found in Luke 11:11–13 RSV. It sounds almost as if our Lord anticipated this very concern.

*What father among you, if his son asks for a fish, will instead of a fish give him a serpent; or if he asks for an egg, will give him a scorpion? If you then, who are evil, know how to give good gifts to your children, **how much more** will the heavenly Father give the Holy Spirit to those who ask him!*

CHAPTER 12

Must a message in tongues in a meeting always be interpreted?

We have already discussed the two ways tongues are to be manifested. The first is praying in tongues—the ability to pray in the Spirit that comes when one received the baptism in the Holy Spirit. There are no limitations on this private, personal use of tongues. It is a powerful instrument for strengthening and edifying yourself spiritually. This is apparent when we see that praying in tongues is praying *"in the Spirit."*

> *Pray at all times **in the Spirit,** with all prayer and supplication.* (Ephesians 6:18 RSV)

> *But you, beloved, build yourselves up on your most holy faith; **pray in the Holy Spirit**.* (Jude 20 RSV)

Neither is there any limitation on tongues when it is used as the corporate expression of worship. In the book of Acts, where various groups of Christians were filled with the Spirit and began to speak in tongues, there were no restrictions or limitations placed on this free expression of worship. (See Acts 2:4; 10:46; 19:6.) All received the Spirit and were praying in tongues out loud and at the same time. It was corporate praise.

But the same Paul who prayed for the twelve Ephesian disciples to receive the Holy Spirit and who watched them pray in tongues, all out loud and at the same time (see Acts 19:6) gave instructions that tongues manifested in a meeting should be interpreted and that only two or three should speak at a time. (See 1 Corinthians 12:27.) This is the second of the two ways tongues are manifested—as a gift of tongues to be followed by interpretation.

Therefore, we see that in a meeting, at any time other than private prayer or corporate worship in the Spirit, speaking in tongues should be followed by interpretation, that the church may be edified. In such cases, interpretation is not only in order, it's mandatory.

The confusion in the minds of some people over what is a manifestation of tongues in worship and what is the gift of tongues to be interpreted can be seen in this illustration. In California last year, I addressed a large congregation in a downtown San Francisco auditorium. At the close of the service, some fifty people came backstage for prayer to receive the baptism in the Holy Spirit. The Spirit moved quickly over the group, and soon most were praising God in other tongues.

As I moved around listening to some and encouraging others, I came up behind an earnest young man whom I thought at first was one of the local elders who had been assigned to help. To my surprise, he was rather desperately laying his hands on the heads of two people who were speaking in tongues.

"Now stop speaking in tongues and interpret! Don't pray in tongues any more until you've interpreted what you said. Pray for interpretation!" As it happened, the two people he was talking to were so caught up in the Spirit that they were blissfully unaware of his presence. I touched him on the shoulder.

"Don't bother them; just let them enjoy worshipping the Lord."

The young man took me to one side. "Let me show you something," he whispered fiercely, and began thumbing frantically through his Bible. Then finding the Scripture, he shoved his Bible under my nose.

"Read that!" he exclaimed. "Then you'll understand what I was doing!" The verse he was pointing to was 1 Corinthians 14:27: *"If any speak in a tongue, let there be only two or at most three, and each in turn; and let one interpret."*

I smiled at the young Christian's earnestness. He was sure we were completely "out of order" because all the newly-baptized Christians were worshipping in tongues simultaneously.

"But don't you see?" I answered. "This Scripture doesn't apply in this situation. These people are receiving their own personal Pentecost." And I quickly explained the difference between tongues at the point of receiving the baptism in the Spirit and the gift of tongues to be interpreted. When the truth of what I was saying finally dawned, he shook his head in relief.

"I just didn't want us to be doing anything that was unscriptural," he said.

We weren't.

CHAPTER 13

Can you give some modern examples where speaking in
tongues proved to be in a language understood by the hearers?

Incidents where speaking in tongues is recognized by someone listening as a foreign language unknown to the speaker
are always thrilling. They are clearly miraculous manifestations of the power of God. And such stories are an important
and inspiring part of the evidence of what God is doing by the
power of His Spirit today. Nearly every book dealing with the
reality of speaking in tongues gives at least one or two such
illustrations. We are happy to add a few more to the increasing
evidence.

American Baptist Pastor Prays in Japanese

During a week of charismatic seminars conducted in the state
of Kansas, I was teamed up with pastor Ernie Gruen, a spirit-
baptized American Baptist preacher. One afternoon as we were
praying for some people, I heard Ernie Gruen speaking fluently
and clearly in what was obviously an Asian language. Later I said,
"Ernie, your prayer language sounds like Chinese."

Ernie's face broke into a broad smile. "Japanese," he corrected.
"And people who know Japanese have heard me using it and afterward told me exactly what I said in the prayer."

One such person was Father Robert Arrowsmith, a Spirit-baptized Roman Catholic priest, who had taught in a college in Japan for many years and was very familiar with the Japanese language. I was later in some meetings with Father Arrowsmith and asked him about Ernie Gruen.

"It was one of the most amazing things I have witnessed in my entire Christian experience," Father Arrowsmith admitted. "There I was, in this service with Ernie where we were praying for the sick, when all at once, Ernie, with his midwestern drawl, sounding like something right off the Kansas prairies, suddenly began praying in flawless Japanese. I just stood there and listened in amazement.

"And it happened not just once while I was with him, but on three different occasions."

Disciples of Christ Minister Speaks Spanish

This second illustration is a word of personal testimony. At a meeting of the Cleveland chapter of the Full Gospel Businessmen's Fellowship International, I was praying for a group of people to receive the baptism in the Holy Spirit. There were about seventy people in the prayer room, in addition to those who were helping me minister. Following my usual course, I gave some instruction, and we entered into a time of prayer during which most of those seeking received. As I moved around the room, praying with and encouraging various individuals, I noticed a young man looking at me rather curiously. For a few minutes he followed me around as I ministered.

As the prayer time ended, he spoke to me. "I thought you might be interested to know that I could understand part of what you were saying when you were praying in tongues, encouraging the others. As you were moving from person to person, praying with them in tongues, I heard you speaking Spanish. You were saying over and over, "I will praise Him. I will praise Him."

Of course, I had had no conscious awareness that anything I was saying in tongues was in a known language, but was most grateful for the confirmation that what had happened to so many others had also happened to me. In the Spirit, I had prayed in a tongue unknown to me but recognized by one listening.

A Georgia Teacher Speaks Cherokee Dialect

Rufus Moseley, a Christian saint and mystic who contributed much to my spiritual growth in earlier years, once told me that while speaking in a church in Oklahoma, he had paused to spend a few moments praising God in tongues before continuing with his message. After the service, a Cherokee Indian told him that one of the languages he had been praising God with was the Cherokee Indian dialect, and that Rufus had said in Cherokee, "My God knows me."

Assembly of God Minister Prays in Maori Dialect

When I was in New Zealand in June of 1970, I learned of two miraculous incidents involving tongues and interpretation. The first had taken place when Rev. Charles Simpson, a Baptist preacher and Bible teacher with whom I frequently minister, had been in New Zealand some months previously. In one of Charles' meetings, a man had stood and given a message in tongues that Charles interpreted from the pulpit. Afterward, a Christian Maori (the Maoris were the native population of New Zealand before the English came and still represent a strong minority group in the country) testified that the man who had brought the message in tongues had been speaking the Maori dialect and that Charles Simpson had given an accurate translation in English of what the man had said in Maori. But neither Charles nor the man speaking in tongues had any natural knowledge of the Maori language.

An even more unusual incident in that same country involved two New Zealand pastors, who personally shared the story with me. They had been ministering in prayer to some people seeking the baptism in the Holy Spirit. Among the seekers was a Maori Indian Christian who could speak practically no English and could not understand the instructions and encouragement of those ministering to him.

Suddenly, one of the ministers began speaking in tongues as he laid hands on the Maori brother. The Indian Christian began to smile and nod his head with some excitement, and a few moments later opened his mouth and burst forth speaking in tongues.

The other minister, who could speak and understand Maori, explained what had happened. Al, who could speak no Maori naturally, had begun supernaturally to speak the Maori language. More than that, he was actually giving instructions in Maori, to the Indian, on how to receive the baptism in the Holy Spirit. And having understood the instructions on receiving them in his own language, the Indian had opened his mouth and begun to speak in tongues.

As he concluded the story, the other minister said to me, "The most amazing part of the story is that Al was giving practically word for word in Maori, the same instructions on how to receive the baptism in the Holy Spirit as he gives when he teaches in English."

SECTION III

TONGUES AND INTERPRETATION

"Therefore, he who speaks in a tongue should pray for the power to interpret."
—1 Corinthians 14:13 RSV

CHAPTER 14

What is the gift of interpretation?

The proper full name for the gift is "interpretation of tongues." I make this point simply to stress the need for accuracy in definition. There is a tendency among some Christians to blur or confuse the definition of the spiritual gifts by improper designation. People will sometimes say, "I don't know how to interpret what he said," or "1 don't know how to interpret this situation." And then they will add, "What we need is the gift of interpretation."

No, they don't. They may need spiritual insight or understanding, or perhaps even the gift of "a word of knowledge" or "a word of wisdom," but there is no "gift of interpretation."

The gift of "interpretation of tongues" is the companion gift to the gift of tongues. The two cannot function properly without each other. When the gift of tongues is manifested in a meeting, it is to be followed by the gift of interpretation of tongues, which means giving in English the meaning of the message that has been spoken in tongues.

Since a congregation worshipping in the Spirit would not, in most cases, have people present who could understand naturally what is spoken in tongues, and since the purpose of the operation of spiritual gifts in a meeting is for the edification of the whole church, Paul said,

He who prophesies is greater than he who speaks in tongues, unless some one interprets, so that the church may be edified.
(1 Corinthians 14:5 RSV)

Therefore, he who speaks in a tongue should pray for the power to interpret. (1 Corinthians 14:13 RSV)

Just as speaking in tongues is a completely supernatural manifestation of the Holy Spirit, so is the gift of interpretation of tongues. It is speaking by inspiration of the Holy Spirit in the known language of the assembled worshippers (and for us, this means English) the meaning of what was spoken previously through the manifestation of the gift of tongues.

As we have already seen in Chapter 13, sometimes the gift of interpretation proves to be an exact translation of what is said in tongues. But this is not always true. Interpretation does not necessarily mean translation.

CHAPTER 15

*How can an interpretation of tongues be genuine when it
is three or four times as long as the message in tongues that
precedes it?*

This question expresses a real concern of people who are trying
to understand the operation of spiritual gifts. It is also used by
those seeking to discredit or reject the charismatic gifts in the
church today.

In a meeting recently, the man presiding said, "Let us wait
quietly and see if God will speak to us." After a few moments,
a woman began speaking in tongues. It was one short phrase,
repeated several times, and the whole message lasted no more than
fifteen seconds. Then a man began to speak in English. "Thus saith
the Lord, I am here tonight to bless and strengthen my people.
Give heed to the Lord thy God to walk carefully in His way..." He
continued in that vein for a full minute and a half.

After the interpretation of tongues, the man presiding said,
"For the benefit of those present for the first time, you have just
witnessed the operation of two of the spiritual gifts; the gift of
tongues followed by the gift of interpretation of tongues."

But the incident did not end there. After the meeting, a man
spoke to me. "Brother Basham," he began, "I need your help. I

brought a minister to the meeting tonight. It was his first charis-matic meeting, and he'd never witnessed the manifestation of spir-itual gifts before. But he's nobody's fool, and he told me flatly just now that he cannot accept what he heard as genuine. At least, not the interpretation that followed the tongues. He said the tongues were repetitive and brief, and since the so-called interpretation of tongues contained no repetition and was many times longer, it obviously could not have been the interpretation of the tongues. Brother Basham, what can I tell him?"

There are two possible explanations. The first we touched on at the close of Chapter 14 when we said that interpretation of tongues is not necessarily translation of tongues. Perhaps the best way to explain this is with an illustration.

Suppose you and I were standing in an art gallery looking at a painting, and someone asked each of us to "interpret" the picture. Your interpretation might go something like this:

"Well, it's a nice landscape; with snowcapped mountains in the background, a blue lake in the foreground, rimmed with ever-green trees. And there is sunlight on the water. I believe the artist wanted to depict a feeling of peace; everything in the picture looks so serene, I wish I were there."

That would be a fair and valid interpretation of the paint-ing. Then it is my turn. You don't know this, but I was a com-mercial artist before I decided to enter the Christian ministry. I was trained in color and design and in art appreciation. I agree with you about the mountains and trees and sunlight on the water, and with your interpretation that the artist was depicting a feeling of peace. But that is just the beginning of my interpretation. I go on to describe the means the artist used to accomplish his objec-tive; the organization of the picture—how the eye is led pleasantly around from mountains to trees to sunlit water. I describe the art-ist's brush stroke and the combination of colors he used, and even suggest how his work may have been influenced by other landscape painters.

In other words, my interpretation of that painting might be far more detailed than yours, *but what we both said is true.*

Personal experience confirms this principle in regard to interpretation of tongues. I have been in meetings where I received the interpretation of a message in tongues, but before I could speak, someone else beat me to it. And his interpretation, although not identical with what I had been given, contained the same thought. Had I spoken first, I would have expressed myself somewhat differently to bring essentially the same message. Yet neither his interpretation nor mine would have necessarily been a word-for-word translation of the message in tongues.

But I believe there is an even more common reason for the discrepancy between a short message in tongues and a long interpretation. I believe that many times what passes for tongues followed by interpretation is not that at all; it is tongues followed by prophecy.

We usually assume that the gift of tongues is a message from God addressed to man, and that the interpretation gives us the meaning of God's message in our own language. I'm sure that many times this is true. But this "God-speaking-to-man-through-tongues-and-interpretation" principle omits a fact that Paul made clear in Scripture. At times, *tongues is prayer addressed to God.*

> *For one who speaks in a tongue speaks not to men but to*
> *God.*   (1 Corinthians 14:2 RSV)

> *If I pray in a tongue, my spirit prays.*
>   (1 Corinthians 14:14 RSV)

So if tongues are prayer addressed to God, then any genuine interpretation of them must also be in the form of a prayer addressed to God. I've been present when just that happened. It was recognized that a beautiful, Spirit-inspired English prayer was the interpretation of a prayer in tongues that had just preceded it.

But in most cases, it is assumed that both the message in tongues and the interpretation that follows are God speaking to man. No wonder then, that doubts arise about a short message in tongues followed by a long English interpretation!

Now let's apply the principle of prayer in tongues followed by prophecy to the situation we described at the beginning of the chapter. A brief, repetitive-sounding message in tongues was followed by a lengthy prophetic exhortation believed by most to be an "interpretation of tongues" but by others to be spurious because of its excessive length.

We know it is the purpose of God to bless His people and that those blessings are often withheld until we ask for them in faith. And Scripture tells us we need the Holy Spirit's help to pray in the right way.

> *Likewise the Spirit helps us in our weakness; for we do not know how to pray as we ought, but the Spirit himself intercedes for us with sighs too deep for words. And he who searches the hearts of men knows what is the mind of the Spirit, because* **the Spirit intercedes for the saints according to the will of God.** (Romans 8:26-27 RSV)

God wants to speak, so how does it come to pass? By the Spirit He prompts the woman to offer a prayer in tongues. The translation of it might have been something like this: "Oh God, speak to us! Reveal yourself to your people. Speak to your people tonight!"—a Spirit-inspired, repetitive-sounding prayer. Then in *prophecy* (not interpretation of tongues), God answers the Spirit-inspired prayer. He speaks to His people. "Thus saith the Lord, I am with you tonight to bless and strengthen My people..." The prayer in tongues is a request for God to speak; the prophecy God's answer to the prayer. Not tongues and interpretation but tongues and prophecy.

Someone will ask, "Couldn't God just use prophecy without tongues?" Certainly. Many times prophecy comes without a prior message in tongues.

But let me suggest two additional reasons for tongues preceding prophecy. When the gift of tongues is manifested, there is often an immediate response in the meeting. The tongues seem to galvanize a spiritual expectancy and receptivity. People know they are about to hear from heaven. In such instances, tongues seem to serve as a kind of divine, "May I have your attention, please?" They create a climate where God's revelation will be received eagerly and reverently.

Another reason is that tongues often provide the needed encouragement to one who has a word from the Lord but is reluctant to speak out. I have experienced this very reluctance. Timid or unsure that what I had been given was from the Holy Spirit, I resorted to putting out a fleece. I've said silently, "Lord, I think this is something I should speak out, yet I'm not certain. But if someone speaks in tongues, I know I can interpret."

I can recall at least three distinct occasions when *immediately* after I said those words, someone began to speak in tongues aloud, and I followed with the interpretation or prophecy. With more courage, I could have prophesied without the message in tongues.

So whether it is prayer in tongues followed by prophecy, or a message in tongues followed by interpretation of tongues, either way God uses the combination of tongues followed by English to bless His people.

CHAPTER 16

I speak in tongues privately but have never had the gift of tongues where someone interpreted. How can I know when I'm supposed to do that?

The principle behind the operation of the gifts of the Holy Spirit is faith. There is no progress in the Christian life except by faith. We noted back in Chapter 5 how only one out of seven Spirit-baptized Christians were moving in the gifts of the Holy Spirit. Most others would like to, and they *can,* through the exercise of their faith.

The usual progression from devotional tongues into the inspirational gifts seems to be first, the gift of tongues, then the gift of interpretation of tongues, then the gift of prophecy. The gift of tongues seems to come as the first step beyond praying in tongues. I know few Christians who ever manifested the gift of interpretation of tongues without first manifesting the gift of tongues. This seems logical since the physical process of speaking in tongues is the same, whether it is praying in the Spirit or the gift of tongues that must be followed by interpretation. It is merely the circumstances under which the tongues are to be spoken that determine the category.

But the problem is this: how can a person praying silently in a meeting know whether he's to continue to pray quietly in tongues or to speak out loud in tongues, manifesting the gift of tongues, which is to be followed by interpretation? Paul said,

> *If any speak in a tongue, let there be only two or at most three,*
> *and each in turn; and let one interpret. But if there is no one*
> *to interpret, let each of them keep silence in church and speak*
> *to himself and to God.*   (1 Corinthians 14:27–28 RSV)

Paul was saying that if there is no one to interpret, tongues shouldn't be spoken out loud as the *gift* of tongues, but only silently, in prayer. But if you do feel led to speak in tongues aloud (that is, to manifest the gift of tongues), how can you be sure there will be an interpretation?

There is only one way to find out, and that is to go ahead and do it and see what happens. Gather up your courage, open your mouth and speak out. The next chapter deals with what happens after that.

CHAPTER 17

*Should I interpret my own message in tongues or should I
expect someone else to interpret?*

According to Scripture, a case can be made for both methods. Paul said, *"Let two or three speak...and let one interpret"* (1 Corinthians 14:27, 29 RSV). Thus, the one speaking in tongues is not necessarily going to be the one to interpret. But Paul also said, *"Therefore, he who speaks in a tongue should pray for the power to interpret"* (1 Corinthians 14:13 RSV). By that statement, it is clear that everyone who uses the gift of tongues should also—sooner or later—use the gift of interpretation.

Suppose then, you feel led to manifest the gift of tongues in a meeting, but when you do no one interprets. What then? From the Scriptures we cited, it seems clear that if no one else interprets your message in tongues, the burden is on you to do it yourself. We'll discuss how to do that in the next chapter.

CHAPTER 18

I feel I would like to interpret tongues but how can I be sure what I say will be from God?

Therefore, he who speaks in a tongue should pray for the power to interpret. (1 Corinthians 14:13 RSV)

We are never told in Scripture to pray for anything that is outside the will of God for us. So we see from this Scripture it *is* God's will for every Christian who speaks in tongues to have the gift of interpretation. Therefore, we know God wants us to attempt interpretation and that He wants us to be successful in that attempt. In all our efforts to move into spiritual gifts, we need to remember that God is with us, encouraging us.

It takes more faith to speak by inspiration of the Holy Spirit in English than it does to speak in tongues, because there is a greater fear that what we say may come from our own consciousness rather than from God. When you were first baptized in the Holy Spirit, you had to overcome your timidity about speaking in tongues. You had to open your mouth and speak out in faith, trusting that the sounds and syllables you uttered were being provided by the Holy Spirit. In other words, you learned to speak in tongues by speaking in tongues. The Holy Spirit, as much as

He desires to minister through us, never forces Himself on us. He doesn't push our mouths open and waggle our tongues and force breath out of our lungs to make us speak. He merely prompts us to speak the utterance He provides.

Just as this is true about speaking in tongues, it is also true about the gift of interpretation of tongues. The only way you will ever interpret tongues is to open your mouth and speak out in English the thoughts you feel the Holy Spirit would have you say in response to the message in tongues.

Most Christians fail to realize how *gentle* the promptings of the Holy Spirit are. He does not *compel* us to manifest a spiritual gift; He very gently *prompts* us. And the promptings can be so slight and so gentle that if we aren't sensitive or if we aren't moving in faith, we will dismiss them as being merely momentary thoughts or impressions of our own minds.

Since His promptings *are* gentle, we often wonder, "Was it the Holy Spirit who dropped that thought in my mind when that person began speaking in tongues, or was it my own imagination?" Then our natural timidity takes over, and we say to ourselves, "Since I can't really be *sure* it was the Holy Spirit, I'll just play it safe and keep quiet. For if I speak out and it isn't from the Spirit, I will be terribly embarrassed. Since I can't be sure, I won't say anything."

That's playing it safe all right! That way you run absolutely no risk at all! It takes very little faith to do nothing!

You say you're not sure the prompting is from God, so you wait. And you wait. How long do you wait? How long until you *are* sure those promptings are from God?

I believe *there is only one way you will ever be sure.* And that way is to try it! Speak in faith what has been given to you—no matter how gentle the prompting—trusting that it is from the

Holy Spirit. It is the application of the same spiritual principle we mentioned before: *There is no progress in the Christian life except by faith.*

Most of us need to reevaluate what is taking place when the gifts of the Holy Spirit come into operation. It is the Holy Spirit moving sovereignly to manifest God's purpose and power among His people. We must learn to be, not passive, but cooperative in yielding ourselves to His Spirit; daring to trust that He is fully capable, not only of providing but also of protecting His supernatural manifestations in us.

He understands when we prove to be less than perfect in our attempts to yield to Him. Suppose some attempt to manifest a gift of the Holy Spirit does fail? Suppose you speak in tongues and no one interprets? Or suppose you attempt an interpretation and you stammer and run out of words before you've adequately expressed the thought you felt God gave you? Have you committed a crime? No! All you did was fall short in a sincere attempt to be obedient to the Spirit, and you are under no condemnation from God because of the attempt.

The Lord's encouragement for us to attempt spiritual gifts is something like parents attempting to teach their child how to walk. You know what Mother and Daddy do when they think Junior should begin to walk unaided. Mother stands in the middle of the room with Junior, allowing him to grasp only her index fingers. Daddy steps a few paces away and begins to beckon to his little son.

"Come on, Junior. Come to Daddy."

Then Mother gently disengages her fingers from Junior's hands. There he stands, all by himself, weaving back and forth, looking uncertainly at Mother, then at Daddy, both feet glued to the floor.

"Come on, Junior," Daddy encourages. "Walk to Daddy. You can do it!"

At this point, Junior has a decision to make. *He can take a step of faith, or he can play it safe.* The first time he probably plays it safe. Without moving his feet, he just sinks slowly to the floor, then scampers on his hands and knees over to Daddy with a big smile on his face. (Are you getting the point about "playing it safe"? About not running any risk?)

But Mother and Daddy are not satisfied to let Junior "play it safe." They set up the whole experiment again. There Junior stands once more; wobbling back and forth while Daddy encourages him to take his first step.

This time he does it! He takes one step. Then he takes another step! Then, trying for that third step, he stumbles. Kerplunk! Down he goes, right on his face. He begins to cry. He's failed. He's tried to walk, and he can't!

So what do Mother and Daddy do? Are they angry? Is Junior condemned? Do they punish him for his failure? Has it all been a terrible mistake? Not at all. It was the genuine love and concern of his parents that exposed Junior to the possibility of falling in the first place. They pick him up and praise him for trying. They console him and tell him everything is all right, there's no harm done, and he'll do better next time. Then they try the whole experiment again.

Junior receives no rebuke and no condemnation. How can he when he is surrounded by his parents' love and encouragement? And they will continue to encourage him to stop playing it safe; to stop crawling. They will encourage him in spite of his failures and faltering attempts, until he succeeds in walking. Why? Because they know their son's destiny calls for him to walk. It is a part of his inheritance as their beloved child.

I think by now you can see the analogy. God's dealing with us in terms of growing into a mature understanding and use of spiritual gifts is something akin to our encouraging our children to walk. And our early efforts at manifesting spiritual gifts are often like Junior's first efforts to walk; faltering and imperfect. Nevertheless, we are right in trying.

And we are under no more criticism and condemnation for those faltering efforts than our own children are for their failure to walk perfectly on the first try. More than that, experience shows that even initial, imperfect attempts at manifesting spiritual gifts can be a blessing to the people who receive them. I know of no greater encouragement to one attempting a determined, if somewhat shaky interpretation of tongues, than for him to discover that in spite of its imperfection and lack of eloquence, it truly spoke to the needs of those who heard it. The one interpreting is pleased, the people who receive it are pleased, and God is pleased, all because an attempt has been made in faith to be obedient to the loving, gentle prompting of the Holy Spirit.

CHAPTER 19

Can you tell us how your experience with interpretation of tongues began?

When I was first baptized in the Holy Spirit, I was still laboring under many of the false impressions that plague people today. Back then we did not have the benefit of sound teaching and instruction about how to receive the baptism in the Holy Spirit. Nor did any one warn me that Satan would try to talk me out of my experience.

Consequently, for many weeks after I was baptized in the Holy Spirit, I questioned whether or not my experience of speaking in tongues was real. I did not understand that speaking in tongues would always be a cooperative venture between me and the Holy Spirit, with me doing the speaking and Him furnishing the words and syllables. I continually felt a little twinge of guilt as I spoke in tongues, that perhaps "it was just *me.*" And I was a long time getting over the feeling.

This had an influence, I'm sure, on my failure to experience interpretation of tongues for over a year after I was baptized in the Holy Spirit. Like many others, I would pray in tongues in my private devotions and earnestly hope for the day when I would miraculously be visited with an interpretation of tongues or prophecy.

I did not have the slightest realization then that God was waiting for me to move in faith into the gift of interpretation the same way I had first stepped out in faith to speak in tongues.

It was during a conference at the Elim Bible Institute in Lima, New York, over a year later, that I gained my first insight into how interpretation of tongues was received, and I am indebted to the president of Elim, Dr. Carlton Spencer, for the explanation and encouragement he gave me. During that conference, for the first time, I opened my mouth *in faith,* and gave an interpretation of a message in tongues. At the time, several of us were praying for a woman who was seeking God's direction for her life. My interpretation contained two statements that were so pertinent to her situation that she began to weep with relief.

Since I had felt foolish and self-conscious when I began to speak, and was quite fearful that what I was saying might be simply the working of my own imagination, I was vastly relieved to receive such a quick confirmation that the interpretation really was of the Holy Spirit and not just "me."

CHAPTER 20

*When should one speak a message in tongues? The moment
he feels prompted? I don't want to quench the Spirit.*

Unfortunately, many confusing and hurtful things have been
done in the name of "Quench not the Spirit." Some enthusias-
tic Christians take that Scripture to mean that whatever they
"feel like doing" in a meeting, they should do. Obviously this
was part of the problem in the church at Corinth. There were
uncontrolled displays of supernatural manifestations of the
Holy Spirit, which led to Paul's instructions about the proper
way to operate the spiritual gifts in church. *"Let all things be done
decently and in order"* (1 Corinthians 14:40) was the summation
of Paul's teaching.

Similar lack of discipline in manifesting the gifts of the Spirit
today leads to similar problems. I was in a meeting where Reverend
David Wilkerson of Teen Challenge was preaching under a powerful anointing of the Holy Spirit. The congregation was giving
him their rapt attention when suddenly a man stood up and began
to speak in tongues in a loud booming voice. David asked him to
sit down. Twice, the man ignored David's request. The third time,
David spoke sternly and with authority, "Brother, shut up and sit
down!" The man sat down, obviously miffed at having been pub-
licly rebuked.

The person next to me whispered, "Why did Reverend Wilkerson do that? That man was bringing a message in tongues. I'm afraid Reverend Wilkerson has quenched the Spirit."

Someone had quenched the Spirit in the meeting all right, but it wasn't David. "I believe it was obvious that I was under the anointing of the Holy Spirit," David explained, *"and the Holy Spirit does not interrupt Himself."* Those assuming that any discipline in the manifestation of the gifts of the Spirit is "quenching the Spirit" would have trouble with David's statement.

Nevertheless, Paul said, *"The spirits of the prophets are subject to the prophets. For God is not the author of confusion, but of peace"* (1 Corinthians 14:32–33). If God is not the author of confusion, who is? Satan is. Strange as it seems, Satan, working through fleshly enthusiasm, can prompt the *misuse* of a genuine spiritual gift. That's what happened at Corinth, the improper manifestation of speaking in tongues, which was leading to confusion and disorder. And that's what happened in David Wilkerson's meeting; the improper manifestation of the gift of tongues that interrupted David's anointed preaching.

The brother who interrupted David was genuinely moved and inspired by David's preaching, but he mistook that inspiration as the moving of the Spirit for him to burst out speaking in tongues. (He didn't want to "quench the spirit"!) His speaking in tongues was genuine but out of place. The proper course of action would have been for him to restrain his enthusiasm until David had finished. Then, if he still felt moved by the Holy Spirit to bring a message in tongues, the timing would have been proper, there would have been an interpretation, and the whole meeting would have benefitted from the manifestation of the spiritual gifts. And Paul's clear admonition, *"Let all things be done decently and in order"* (1 Corinthians 14:40), would have been heeded.

CHAPTER 21

How do you know when you are going to interpret tongues?
What inner indication from the Spirit do you receive?

Let me stress again that the promptings of the Holy Spirit are very gentle. I've never heard a thundering voice in my ear saying, "Thus saith the Lord, stand up and interpret." I'm not saying that such dramatic guidance cannot come; I'm only saying that it has never happened to me like that. And the experiences of most other Christians I know who are operating the gifts of the Holy Spirit indicate it doesn't happen to them like that either.

For me, this prompting comes as a kind of inner quickening or inner awareness. Let us suppose I'm the speaker in a meeting, and at the close of my talk, someone brings a message in tongues. If I am to give the interpretation, I usually am made aware of it by a kind of lift in my spirit; an assurance that God wants me to interpret. I may even be given the content of the interpretation before I begin to speak, although much of the time I do not know what I'm going to say, only that I'm going to say it. On such occasions, when I am already "in the Spirit" by virtue of my teaching or speaking, I have no difficulty at all in obeying that inner witness, that "lift" in my spirit that says I'm to interpret. At such times, it's easy to be obedient.

But on other occasions, I may receive this prompting to bring an interpretation, and it is not nearly so easy to obey. Perhaps I'm feeling self-conscious or may just not feel like I'm "in the Spirit." To be obedient in situations like that seems to require much more courage. It can be a real struggle, and at times I have refused to obey. Of course, I have later regretted it because it meant that something precious was lost to the meeting. Perhaps an illustration may be helpful.

It took place some years ago in a prayer meeting at the Neshannock Presbyterian Church in New Wilmington, Pennsylvania. I was pastoring in nearby Sharon, Pennsylvania, at the time. Often, on Saturday nights, a group of us from Sharon would drive the fifteen miles to New Wilmington to attend the charismatic prayer meeting there.

On this particular Saturday, I had had a very difficult day in my own parish. I felt like Satan had dogged my footsteps all day long. I was discouraged and thoroughly "out of the Spirit." I came to the prayer meeting seeking comfort and inspiration but had no inclination to participate in the meeting apart from sitting quietly and receiving any help that might come my way.

We sang hymns and listened to an inspirational message on tape, then went into a time of prayer. Then the gifts of the Holy Spirit began to operate. Someone sang in the Spirit, then someone else prophesied. Following that, a woman began to speak in tongues in a loud clear voice, and to my dismay I felt this quickening feeling inside and knew I had the interpretation. But I was in no mood to speak out, even though along with the quickening had come the awareness of what I was to say. So I stubbornly refused, saying to myself that God should use someone else in the group who was "with it."

There was a long period of silence while the group waited expectantly. And the longer the silence, the more embarrassed I became. I began to wish I had been obedient, but was still too stubborn to yield. To make matters worse, the pastor, Dr. Victor Dawe suddenly spoke up, "Will the person to whom the Holy Spirit has given the interpretation please speak it forth?" I just stared miserably at the floor.

Then to my vast relief, a friend, Russell Sewall, stood up and gave the interpretation. I was gratified as I noted it contained essentially the same thoughts that had been revealed to me.

But the Holy Spirit had still not let me off the hook. A strong sense of conviction suddenly swept over me as the Holy Spirit seemed to say, "You must confess what you did!" The feeling was so strong that I knew I had to obey. And I wished more fervently than ever that I had been obedient to the first prompting of the Spirit.

So with much embarrassment, I confessed. "I've had a very rough day today," I began with a rationalization to try and ease my sense of guilt. "And I haven't felt the least bit spiritual. I came tonight just wanting to sit here and be quiet. But I have to confess that I'm the one responsible for the embarrassing delay between the message in tongues and the interpretation. I was given the interpretation, even while the message in tongues was still in progress, but was too stubborn to give it. I'm very sorry, and I ask you all to forgive me."

Of course the group did, but I felt only slightly better for having made the confession.

There was an interesting conclusion to the incident. Russell Sewall spoke up. "I'm also relieved at the way things turned out," he said. "Because when the message in tongues began, I waited to see if I had any witness that God wanted me to bring the interpretation. But I received no indication at all that I was the one, so I just sat back and waited. But then the long pause came and everyone began to get embarrassed. It seemed obvious that someone was quenching the Spirit and holding back on the interpretation so I said silently, 'Lord, if you've given the interpretation to someone who won't bring it forth, then let me have it, and I'll give it.' And immediately the Lord quickened the interpretation to me."

It all turned out to be a demonstration of the Lord's loving way of dealing with us, and a somewhat painful lesson to me not to quench the Spirit, but to be obedient, even if I'm not "feeling spiritual."

THE GIFT OF PROPHECY

"Now I want you all to speak in tongues,
but even more to prophesy."
—1 Corinthians 14:5 RSV

CHAPTER 22

*What is the gift of prophecy and how does it differ from the
gift of interpretation?*

Essentially there is one major difference between the gift of interpretation and the gift of prophecy. The gift of interpretation follows a manifestation of the gift of tongues while the gift of prophecy requires no prior message in tongues.

Concerning the value of prophecy, Paul said,

*Now I want you all to speak in tongues, but even more to
prophesy. He who prophesies is greater than he who speaks in
tongues, unless someone interprets, so that the church may be
edified.* (1 Corinthians 14:5 RSV)

It needs to be understood that Paul was not exalting one spiritual gift above another, but merely placing priority on those gifts that edify the *church* because he was writing about a *church* problem, not about an individual problem. In the assembled congregation, Paul said, prophecy is of greater value than tongues since all those hearing the prophecy can understand the meaning of what is said.

Prophecy is a supernatural gift. It is speaking forth by direct inspiration of the Holy Spirit the words of God to His people. It is not merely inspirational or eloquent speaking, as the diluted renderings of the word in some modern translations of the Bible would infer.

CHAPTER 23

Does the gift of prophecy always contain predictions about the future?

This seems to be a common misconception many people have concerning prophecy. But prophecy is not necessarily "foretelling"; it is "forthtelling." It is speaking forth the message of God to His people, and in many—if not most—cases it will *not* contain predictions about the future.

Prediction, while a genuine part of prophecy, is only a small part. Our national preoccupation with astrology, fortune-telling, spiritualism, and the popularity of clairvoyants like Jean Dixon and Edgar Cayce have urged many a Christian into a morbid desire to peek into the future. But Paul told us,

> *He that prophesieth speaketh unto man to edification, and exhortation, and comfort.* (1 Corinthians 14:3)

And in Paul's definition, we see no mention of foretelling the future. However, the gift of prophecy, when it is manifested in a meeting, may contain other revelation, such as the word of knowledge or the word of wisdom.

> *But if all prophesy, and there come in one that believeth not, or one unlearned, he is convinced of all, he is judged of all:*

*and thus are the secrets of his heart made manifest; and so
falling down on his face he will worship God, and report that
God is in you of a truth.* (1 Corinthians 14:24–25)

If prophecy is for *"edification, and exhortation, and comfort,"* it
can contain much revelation and insight from the Lord that will
strengthen and encourage and bless people without predicting a
single future event. Past events or information in the life of a person
not known to the one prophesying are as much a demonstration of
the supernatural nature of prophecy as predicting future events.

Directive prophecy, or predicting the future, can be a valid
manifestation of prophecy, but should be used with only the greatest discretion and should be received with real caution and reserve.
A good rule to follow concerning receiving such prophecy is to
hold it in abeyance until it is confirmed. *"In the mouth of two or
three witnesses shall every word be established"* (2 Corinthians 13:1).

In other words, if you receive two or three prophecies from
different, *independent* sources about some future ministry, then
the word from God has been confirmed and is likely to be genuine.
Or if God has been dealing with you privately about a matter and
then a word of prophecy comes from someone who knows nothing
of the matter, then it is a genuine word of prophecy.

For example, two years ago, God began indicating to me that I
would spend some time ministering in the New England states, a
part of the country I had never visited. I even woke up one morn-
ing praying for the state of Massachusetts. References in the news-
papers mentioning the New England states seemed to catch my
attention.

"I believe I'm going to New England sometime soon," I told my
wife Alice. Sure enough, a few weeks later at a spiritual life semi-
nar, a man from New England told me the Lord had spoken to him
in prophecy to invite me to New England for a series of seminars. I

had little difficulty deciding the prophecy was from the Lord, since the Holy Spirit had been dealing privately with me about just such a ministry. The man's prophecy was confirmation. The seminars were held and proved fruitful.

The main difficulty with prophecies that predict future events or ministries is that they can degenerate into fortune-telling. For this very reason, the Pentecostal movement, which began around the turn of the century with a fairly strong emphasis on personal prophecy, has largely retreated from this emphasis because of the problems and abuses to which it led.

It should be remembered that there is nothing uniquely Christian about predicting the future. Seers, mystics and clairvoyants have been common throughout history, and many of them have amassed a formidable record of success, while having nothing whatever to do with the Christian faith. Such abilities are, of course, of psychic and demonic origin and are not to be confused with the true gift of prophecy springing from the Holy Spirit through the grace of Jesus Christ.

CHAPTER 24

I've heard prophecies that are hard and judgmental.
Are they valid?

Prophecy is often affected by the person through which it comes. Pure water pouring from a rusty pipe will be colored by the rust. The rust is not from the water, but from the pipe. So then, pure prophecy may be delivered in an impure manner. The gift of prophecy, if it is not manifested in love, may lose much of its effectiveness. Paul said,

> *If I speak in the tongues of men and of angels, but have not love, I am a noisy gong or a clanging cymbal. And if I have prophetic powers...but have not love, I am nothing.*
> (1 Corinthians 13:1–2 RSV)

The prophecy may be genuine, but its impact will be diminished and its truth obscured by the unloving way it is brought forth. This is why we need to develop not only the gifts of the Spirit but the fruit of the Spirit as well. They go together. Either without the other is greatly lacking. The one manifesting a gift of prophecy will be far more effective if that prophetic gift springs out of the fruit of love and peace.

But we must remember that God works *through* human personality, not apart from it. And there are no perfect people. Paul said,

"We have this treasure in earthen vessels, to show that the transcendent power belongs to God and not to us" (2 Corinthians 4:7 RSV). The vessels God deigns to pour His Spirit through can be very "earthy."

A man's attitudes and opinions, his theological beliefs and social prejudices, all may color the content of his prophecy. Rufus Moseley used to say, "A narrow-minded man receives a narrow-minded revelation, but a genuine revelation nevertheless." God does accommodate Himself to us for all our weaknesses. Thus, prophecies may seem more harsh and judgmental than God intends, simply because they are reflecting something of the personality through which they come.

Also, genuine prophecy may contain statements of a corrective or chastening nature. In his call to Jeremiah the prophet, God said,

> *Behold, I have put my words in your mouth. See, I have set you this day over nations and over kingdoms, to pluck up and to break down, to destroy and to overthrow, to build and to plant.* (Jeremiah 1:9–10 RSV)

Sometimes a chastening or correcting word from the Lord is needed before the strengthening and upbuilding words can be given. But such correction from the Holy Spirit will normally be followed by the assurance of God's restoration and blessing, once the correcting word has been heeded.

But let us make it clear; *not all prophecy is from God.* If someone you know perpetually prophesies doom and destruction, or if his prophecies consistently instill fear and never strengthen or encourage, then you may be sure his words are not from the Lord.

I know of a woman in a certain Eastern city who claims to be a "prophetess" but whose "word from the Lord" is always negative. Many people in her community have received morbid telephone calls from her.

"Hello, Martha? It's me. Are you all right?"

"Yes, I'm fine."

"Well, what I meant was, are your children still all right? None of them is ill? Or has been injured in an accident or anything?"

"No, they are all fine. Why?"

"Well, I was praying about your family, and I received a word from the Lord and...well, I think you should be very careful the next few days or..."

Such morbidity never originates with the Holy Spirit.

CHAPTER 25

If the gift of prophecy is from God, why must it be judged?

*Love never ends; as for prophecies, they will pass away; as for tongues, they will cease; as for knowledge, it will pass away. For our knowledge is imperfect and **our prophecy is imperfect.*** (1 Corinthians 13:8–9 RSV)

*Let two or three prophets speak, and **let the others weigh what is said.*** (1 Corinthians 14:29)

From these two Scriptures, it is obvious why prophecy is to be judged. It is to be judged because it is imperfect. Unfortunately, many people have had a very naïve concept of spiritual gifts and how they operate in the believer's life. While spiritual gifts are received by grace through faith, this does not alter the basic spiritual principle of growth. As our faith and receptivity increase, the measure of spiritual gifts that can operate safely through us will also increase.

We described in Chapter 18 how moving into spiritual gifts is like Junior learning to walk. His first efforts are uncertain and faltering, and he is bound to fail. He is under no condemnation for his failures, however, because through them he is learning to walk successfully.

When we apply this principle to manifesting the gift of prophecy, we can see how beginnings in prophecy may be small and imperfect; how they may contain thoughts that are not totally God's. That's why Paul said our prophecy is imperfect.

But the answer to the problem is not to discourage prophecy. In fact, we are scripturally forbidden to do that. *"Do not despise prophesying,"* Paul said in 1 Thessalonians 5:20. Have you ever wondered what prompted Paul to write that? What was happening at Thessalonica that would cause those Christians to look down on prophecy? Apparently, some of the prophetic messages were proving less than helpful or less than edifying. They may have been more than imperfect; they may have been downright awful!

I have been in situations more than once where such unsatisfactory manifestations came forth. The person who prophesied was obviously sincere, but the content of the prophecy was so garbled and confused that it lowered the spiritual temperature of the meeting by many degrees. Under such circumstances, one is almost tempted to throw up his hands in despair and give up teaching about spiritual gifts.

But Paul said that is not the answer. *"Do not despise prophesying,"* rather, *"let two or three prophets speak, and let the others weigh what is said."* So what are we to do when prophecy comes that is obviously spurious? We are not to blame the spiritual gift, but to counsel the one who abused it or attempted unsuccessfully to manifest it. He can be commended on his desire to operate the gift, even as he is informed that the content was not up to scriptural standards. It may have simply failed to "edify, exhort, or comfort."

The fact that Paul *insisted* that prophecy should be judged or weighed is clear indication that everything that is uttered as a prophecy is not necessarily from God. Unfortunately, our desire to avoid controversy and hurt feelings often leads us to suffer in silence when some brother or sister prophesies improperly.

I recall a situation where a self-styled prophet was blatantly moving around the room laying hands on people's heads and prophesying much too freely. Many people were embarrassed by his brashness, but no one made a move to stop him until he prophesied over one gentle little fellow who normally would have walked a mile to avoid a confrontation or a controversy. But the little man was somehow emboldened by the Holy Spirit to jump to his feet immediately after the prophecy was spoken over him.

"Brother, I do not receive that prophecy," he said with unusual boldness. "And I do not witness to the validity of your prophetic ministry."

Encouraged by his honesty, others then confirmed that they too had felt offended by his ministry. The effect was something like letting air out of a balloon. The egocentric "prophet" was thoroughly deflated and meekly sat down.

While on the surface, such behavior may have seemed critical and embarrassing, how much better for the problem to be dealt with quickly! Not only was the group saved further embarrassment and possible deception, but the "prophet" himself, having been properly chastened, was in a position to have his intended ministry disciplined and corrected. To have allowed the prophetic farce to continue without challenge would have been unwise, unloving and un-Christian.

We need to recognize, however, that the problem is not always so obvious. What about the prophecy that, although not particularly harmful, simply falls flat? It's dull and uninspiring. Such a case is something like Junior's attempted first step, which ended by him falling on his face.

A proper procedure would be to speak to the person, perhaps privately, expressing appreciation for his attempt, while not endorsing the content of the message.

And what of the prophecy that begins in the Spirit and ends in the flesh? The prophecy begins with eloquence and power, pleasing the people and the prophet. But the prophet gets carried away and continues to speak after the Holy Spirit stops. Those listening know that prophecy has ended in the flesh. Here again, a word to the prophet can be of help.

"I really appreciated that prophecy," you may say, "especially the first part." If the prophet is really wanting to be obedient and submissive, he will understand what you mean.

We should not close our discussion of judging prophecy without mentioning scriptural tests for prophecy. Reverend Derek Prince, a friend and fellow Bible teacher, has written an excellent little booklet called *How to Judge Prophecy*.[2] In it, he lists nine scriptural tests that we summarize here. We recommend his book for a more detailed consideration of this question.

1. The end purpose of all true prophecy is to build up, to admonish, and to encourage the people of God. Anything that is not directed to that end is not true prophecy. (1 Corinthians 14:3)

2. All true prophecy agrees with the letter and the spirit of the Scriptures. (2 Timothy 3:16)

3. All true prophecy centers in Jesus Christ and exalts and glorifies Him. (John 16:13)

4. True prophecy produces fruit in character and conduct that agrees with the fruit of the Holy Spirit. (Galatians 5:22–23)

5. If a prophetic revelation contains predictions concerning the future, are these predictions fulfilled? If not, the revelation is not from God. (Deuteronomy 18:20–22)

2. *How to Judge Prophecy*, Derek Prince Publications, P.O. Box 306, Ft. Lauderdale, FL.

6. The fact that a person makes a prediction concerning the future that is fulfilled does not necessarily prove that that person is a true prophet. If such a person, by his ministry, turns others away from obedience to the one true God, then that person is a false prophet, even if he makes correct predictions concerning the future. (Deuteronomy 13:1–5)

7. True prophecy, given by the Holy Spirit, produces liberty and not bondage. (2 Corinthians 3:7)

8. True prophecy, given by the Holy Spirit, produces life, not death. (2 Corinthians 3:6)

9. True prophecy, given by the Holy Spirit, is attested by the Holy Spirit within each believer who hears it. (1 John 2:27)

It should be obvious that in order for one to judge fairly and correctly the prophecies he hears, he must be knowledgeable about the Scriptures. The only real safety for the Christian lies in knowing and applying God's Word.

CHAPTER 26

*Why do some people who prophesy
shout or wail when they speak?*

This is a concern of many Christians who come from formal church backgrounds. Denominations such as the Presbyterian, Methodist, and Episcopal have certain traditions in worship that are quite different from Pentecostal or Holiness traditions. One group tends toward formality, the other toward spontaneity.

A Methodist goes to a freewheeling Pentecostal service and comes away complaining, "They're too emotional," while the Pentecostal visiting a formal service in a Methodist church comes away saying with a shake of his head, "They're dead."

In some Pentecostal traditions, where loud praise and shouting are considered evidences of the Spirit's moving rather than signs of emotionalism, the high-pitched prophetic utterance is considered normal.

But today, as old-line Pentecostals are coming together in charismatic meetings with Spirit-baptized Christians from mainline denominations, the loud booming voice or wailing cry of the prophesying Pentecostal can be a real distraction.

We should remember that the Holy Spirit is quite able to communicate through people who speak in a normal tone of voice.

We need not be critical of those who manifest genuine gifts of the Spirit out of their own noisier traditions, but God does not expect nor intend us to mimic their methods.

CHAPTER 27

*Can you give us some examples of prophecies that had an
effect on your own life?*

One of the first prophecies destined to have an effect on my
life happened nearly twenty years ago. My wife and I were trou-
bled over whether or not I should continue training in Bible college. I had given up a budding career in commercial art to enter
the ministry, but the intellectual barrenness of Bible college
was such a contrast to the spiritual vitality we had discovered
through the baptism in the Holy Spirit that I was having second
thoughts.

Between semesters, we sought the counsel of Christian friends
who strengthened and encouraged us. One prophesied over me,
saying that my formal religious training would one day prove to be
like Saul's armor that he tried to put on David before his contest
with Goliath.

"The time will come when you will discover that Saul's armor
will not fit you," the prophecy stated. "And you will discard it
to move out like the boy David, armed only with a sling and the
smooth stones of the Word of God."

Fifteen years passed before that prophecy came true. When I
was confronted with the decision to leave the pastoral ministry for

the life of faith, that prophecy was one of the confirming signs that the step that led to my present ministry was the right one.

A second prophecy that had special significance for me came just before I left the pastorate. At a small Full Gospel church my wife and I were visiting, the minister and elders had gathered around us to pray. To my surprise, the pastor prophesied that I would be led into a ministry of casting out demons. At the time, I had scarcely been exposed to the reality of the deliverance ministry and had practically no experience in it. And as we left the meeting, a stranger came up to share with us a vision of his. He said he had seen me in a great meeting, telling people of the authority of Jesus Christ, and then I had begun to cast out evil spirits. His statement was confirmation of the prophecy I had received (unknown to him!) minutes earlier. Not long after those incidents, I found myself involved in situations that called for the ministry of deliverance. The prophecy and vision were strengthening factors in my willingness to enter this controversial ministry.

A third prophecy is one that came through me personally. It contained a supernatural word of knowledge that proved to be an encouraging word for several of us who were in a very unusual situation.

Through a strange set of circumstances, a little over two years ago, I found myself joined to a small but dedicated band of Christians embarked on a risky journey in behind the Iron Curtain to smuggle in a load of Christian literature to the believers in Yugoslavia and Hungary. Clearing the border with our load of spiritual contraband intact, we deposited several hundred Yugoslavian Bibles in that country and after a few days of fellowship with Christians there, headed for the Hungarian border. Again clearing customs safely, we made our way to Budapest and checked into a hotel.

Frankly, it is a creepy experience to be in a country where Christians are considered enemies of the government, and where your sole reason for being there is to pray for and encourage those very "enemies."

Feeling somewhat uneasy and forlorn, we sat in our hotel room praying for the meeting we would be attending that night. For me, America seemed awfully far away. I found myself wondering, "Basham, what on earth are you doing in a strange place like this?"

Our team consisted of an English publisher and his wife, an English architect, an American missionary stationed in Austria, and myself. As we prayed and waited before the Lord, I heard myself begin to prophesy. In the prophecy, the Lord indicated that he had drawn the five of us together from our divergent walks of life to make this particular journey for a particular reason. That much of the prophecy sounded fine. But then I heard my own lips add these words. "I have called you together for this trip and for this ministry, *to take the place of others I called but who failed to go.*"

Frankly, I was astonished. I couldn't help but wonder if the words had really been from God, or were just from some quirk in my own imagination. Then there were some additional words of encouragement and comfort about the success and continuing benefits that would follow our ministry.

We visited a small church that night, and speaking through interpreters, had the opportunity to share teaching and testimony with the Hungarian Christians. Their deep pleasure and gratitude over our coming to encourage them in their difficult situation was humbling to us all.

After the meeting, the missionary member of our team rushed up to me in some excitement. "I've just received confirmation about something God said to us in the prophecy this afternoon," he said.

"You remember how surprised you were at the word that the Lord had sent us to take the place of others who had refused to go?" I nodded.

"Well, I was just talking to an elderly gentleman who some time ago visited his son who lives in the United States. While there, he met two young missionaries who told him they had been called by the Lord to Hungary. He returned home with the news that American missionaries were coming to teach and encourage them. But with tears in his eyes he just now told me, 'They never came. We waited but they never came.' And then he said to me with a smile, 'But you came, and we're so grateful!'

"I know," the missionary concluded, "that God led him to tell me that story so we would know that what was said in the prophecy this afternoon was really from the Lord."

I gratefully agreed with my missionary friend. The confirmation of the word of knowledge contained in that prophecy encouraged us all. *"He who prophesies,"* Paul said, *"speaks to men for their edification, and exhortation, and comfort."* And the five of us ministering for a few days in that darkened country where the gospel is considered a political threat and where Christians meet for prayer at great personal risk, knew exactly what Paul meant.

ABOUT THE AUTHOR

Don Basham (1926—1991) was born and reared in Wichita Falls, Texas. As a young man, he left a promising career as a commercial artist in that city to enter the ministry. Basham held degrees from Phillips University and its Graduate Seminary in Enid, Oklahoma, and was an ordained minister of the Christian Church (Disciples of Christ).

Basham served as pastor in churches in Washington, D.C.; Toronto, Canada; and Sharon, Pennsylvania. He also served as editor of *New Wine*, an international magazine dedicated to Christian growth, for a time while living in Mobile, Alabama, with his wife Alice and their children. He was involved in writing, counseling, and teaching in both national and international speaking engagements.